HOW TO
PLAY SAXOPHONE
John Robert Brown

St. Martin's Press
New York

HOW TO PLAY SAXOPHONE. Copyright © 1983 by International
Music Publications. All rights reserved. Printed in the United
States of America. No part of this book may be used or
reproduced in any manner whatsoever without written
permission except in the case of brief quotations embodied
in critical articles or reviews. For information, address St.
Martin's Press, 175 Fifth Avenue, New York, N.Y. 10010.

Library of Congress Cataloging-in-Publication Data

Brown, John Robert.
    How to play saxophone / John Robert Brown.
      p. cm.
    ISBN 0-312-10477-4
    1. Saxophone—Instruction and study. I. Title.
MT500.B76 1994
788.7′193—dc20   93-33497
                                                    CIP
                                                    MN

First published in Great Britain by Elm Tree Books Ltd.

First U.S. Edition: January 1994
10 9 8 7 6 5 4 3 2 1

Contents

Introduction

HOW TO USE THIS BOOK

This guide is written to help you from the second or third year of playing onwards, when you will already have a knowledge of the fundamentals of music notation, can read a simple tune at sight, and have learned the conventional fingerings for the standard range of the saxophone. It is intended to be particularly useful to those who have already enjoyed a firm grounding playing the clarinet or flute.

The aims of the book are:

1) To revise what you have learned so far.

2) To help speed you on to the standard required for professional playing by suggesting some time saving approaches.

3) To help you produce a good personal sound.

4) To learn the fundamentals behind different rhythmic styles.

5) To help develop your improvising skills.

6) To offer some guidance with advanced techniques such as *double-densities* and high notes beyond the traditional normal range.

In such a book as this it isn't possible to include nearly enough practice material, and it is assumed that you will find appropriate supplementary exercises to augment the material given.

HOW TO PLAY SAXOPHONE may be used as a conventional tutor for you to work through chapter by chapter. For instance, the book is carefully organised to ensure that by the time you have worked to the end of chapter three you will have revised all the conventional major and minor scales in all keys. It is also hoped that the book will prove to be a long-term companion for the serious saxophonist. Features such as the double-density chart, the high-note fingering chart and the repertoire lists and bibliography are provided for reference throughout your playing and teaching career.

Note:
Many of the tunes in this book have chord symbols included, so that you can organise some guitar or piano accompaniment for yourself. The chords are given in the same key as the melody. The part for the accompanist will have to be transposed to suit the pitch of the saxophone you play.

The Saxophone Family

The saxophone was invented in the mid-nineteenth century by a Belgian instrument maker, Adolphe Sax. His patent for the saxophone was filed in 1846. The complete story is told in *Adolphe Sax 1814 — 1894: his life and legacy,* by Wally Horwood[1].

The family of saxophones in common use today is as follows:

Soprano in B♭
Range *(sounding):*   *written:*

   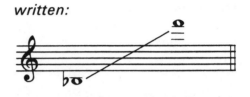

Alto in E♭
Range `(sounding):*`   *written:*

Tenor in B♭
Range *(sounding):*   *written:*

Baritone in E♭
Range *(sounding):*   *written:*

   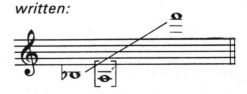

There are other less frequently-used members of the saxophone family. The **Eb Sopranino** saxophone is pitched an octave above the alto. This is one of the instruments used in the score of Ravel's *Bolero*. As the part lies within the range of the Bb soprano, however, it is usually transposed and played on the lower instrument. The **C Melody** saxophone enjoyed brief popularity before the Second World War. As its name suggests, it is pitched in C, a tone above the tenor saxophone. It has a pleasant, light sound, though it is rarely heard today. The **Bass** saxophone is an octave below the tenor. It has exceptional mobility for such a low instrument. Again, it is a member of the saxophone family that is not frequently encountered, but it may sometimes be heard as a fourth member in the front line of twenties-style jazz bands.

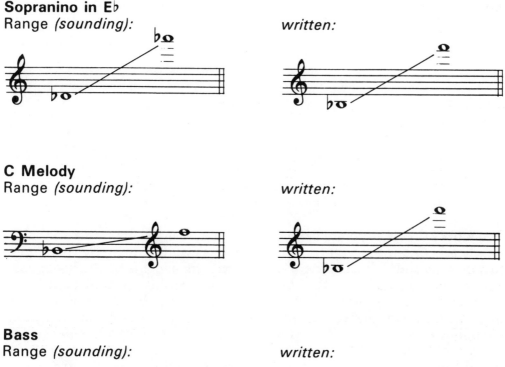

Sopranino in Eb
Range *(sounding):*   *written:*

C Melody
Range *(sounding):*   *written:*

Bass
Range *(sounding):*   *written:*

Mention must also be made of rarities such as the **Eb Contrabass,** the **Mezzo-Soprano** in F, the **Swanee** saxophone (fitted with a slide like a Swanee whistle) and the **Saxie,** a keyless simplified novelty.

POPULARITY AND ACCEPTANCE

Wide acceptance of the saxophone came with the twentieth century. It's interesting to note that Elgar seriously considered employing a quartet of saxophones in *Caractacus* (1898) but was dissuaded from doing so 'because of the problems attached to the finding of suitable players and the expense of rehearsing them' [2]. Debussy's *Rapsodie* appeared in 1911, but it was during and after the popular saxophone craze of the 1920's that the saxophone also began to appear in the instrumentation of new orchestral pieces. A comprehensive list of 'serious' repertoire for the saxophone is given in *125 Ans de Musique pour Saxophone* by Jean-Marie Londeix.[3] This book covers around 3,000 titles by 1,000 composers. Among the best known items in the orchestral repertoire which use a saxophone in the instrumentation are:

Berg, *Violin Concerto*
Bizet, *L'Arlesienne Suites,* Nos. 1 and 2
Britten, *Sinfonia da Requiem*
Gershwin, *An American in Paris*
Kodaly, *Háry Janos* Suite
Mussorgsky-Ravel, *Pictures at an Exhibition*
Prokovief, *Lieutenant Kijé*
Ravel, *Bolero*
Strauss, *Domestic Symphony*
Stravinsky, *Ebony Concerto*
Vaughan Williams, *Job* and *Symphony No. 9*
Walton, *Façade* and *Belshazzar's Feast*

The works that feature the saxophone as a *solo* instrument in a concerto nearly all concentrate on the Eb alto, most notably those by Glazunov, Ibert, D'Indy and Debussy. There is a concerto for soprano by H. Villa-Lobos. The tenor and baritone fare badly in the quantity of solo orchestral material written for them. In the world of dance bands and jazz, the alto and tenor have always been the most popular saxophones, the saxophone section in a big band eventually settling to a conventional instrumentation of two altos, two tenors and a baritone. This was so much the rule that arrangers and composers who were the exception frequently ended up with a sound particularly their own, examples being the popular clarinet-led section sound associated with Glen Miller (Clrt., A,A,T,T), the 'Four Brothers' sound of Guiffre/Herman (T,T,T,B), and the soprano-led section used so well by Thad Jones (S,A,T,T,B). From the 1960's onwards there has been renewed interest in the soprano, and this in turn has aided the revival of interest in the saxophone quartet. The sound of the quartet has been well received. 'Next to the string quartet, a quartet of saxophones provides what is perhaps the most satisfying blend of kindred instruments' is the opinion of Sax's biographer Wally Horwood.[4] The saxophone quartet (S,A,T,B) now has a large and varied repertoire, though many would say that it still awaits a first-rate work by a first-rate composer.

CHOOSING WHICH SAXOPHONE TO PLAY

You may not have decided which saxophone to purchase — soprano, alto, tenor or baritone. **The best reason for playing any instrument is because you like the sound it makes.** Generally speaking, the higher (smaller) the saxophone the more difficult it is to control, and the more exposed you are in the ensemble. If you already play a little, and seek the fun and experience of ensemble playing with players who are more competent than you, then one of the lower saxophones may be preferred, offering you the chance to play along in good company in a not-too-conspicuous role. If you want to play the saxophone with a wide repertoire of music of all types, then the alto is first choice, with tenor second. If you are a good clarinet player, with a well-developed embouchure, you *should* be equipped to tackle the soprano — though the embouchures of clarinet and soprano are *not* the same. The repertoire of the soprano is still patchy. It is used in the French saxophone quartet of course (the American quartet uses A,A,T,B) but very little in the orchestra, only occasionally in stage bands, hardly ever in the wind (Military) band.

The fact that the saxophone is a transposing instrument, and the relative merits of playing an instrument in B♭ or E♭, are often considered to be major factors by those choosing which of the family to play. Be assured that these aspects of transposition become relatively unimportant once you have been playing for a while. Finally, when weighing the factors affecting your decision on which member of the saxophone family to play, DO seek the opinion of an experienced saxophonist if at all possible.

BUYING A SAXOPHONE

A secondhand saxophone of post-war vintage and reputable make may well be a better instrument (and cheaper) than a new instrument by an obscure maker. Find out which makes of saxophones today's good players are using, and if possible persuade a friendly experienced player, or your teacher, to play your prospective purchase. TRY BEFORE YOU BUY! Check the pitch and intonation. (*Intonation* is the term used to describe the accuracy of the tuning of the instrument *relative to itself*). You can check the pitch by using a tuning fork or an electronic tuning device such as a Korg tuner or a Stroboconn. Look for damage to the body of the saxophone — bad dents at the narrower end of the bore, broken solder joints, patches, corrosion. Broken springs or worn pads are relatively minor faults compared with damage to the body and keywork. Pads and springs are easily replaced, but this involves expense, and may be the basis of some useful haggling for a price reduction. Saxophones are usually sold complete with case. New ones are usually supplied with sling and mouthpiece as well. Check that the crook and body are of the same make and model. A change of crook makes a considerable difference to the blowing characteristics of a saxophone. In this respect it is a helpful development by at least one manufacturer that their latest models are now available with a choice of four crooks.

CARE AND MAINTENANCE

To tell a beginner to 'leave well alone' in the matter of *routine* maintenance may seem strange advice, but there seems to be as much damage done to instruments by the owner tampering, or being over-attentive, as there is by neglect. Oil should be used very sparingly on rods and keys (keep it away from pads) and apart from an occasional wipe with a duster a saxophone needs very little regular attention. Keep the mouthpiece, crook and the upper body clean internally, both for reasons of hygiene and to avoid the distorted blowing characteristics caused by the altered dimensions of the bore. It makes good sense to replace damaged pads and springs quickly. Makeshift repairs have a tendency to cause further trouble if left in place for long. For example, rubber bands used as substitute 'springs' tend to mark the lacquer if left in place for a long while.

Even when practising at home, it is advisable to replace your saxophone in its case between your work periods. Out of its case and unattended it's a *very* vulnerable piece of equipment.

With use, the cork on the crook will shrink, and the mouthpiece will become a loose fit. The cork can be expanded by gentle heating with a match or cigarette lighter. This will extend its useful life by several months. Heating with a flame is far quicker to carry out than the alternative method of packing with strips of paper or binding with thread, and gives a better end result.

EQUIPMENT

SLINGS need to be comfortable, and not to slip or break. For the baritone saxophone you'll need a wide sling — about 5 cms. wide — to spread the weight of the instrument and prevent discomfort. The curved soprano needs a very short sling. Specially designed ones are supplied with new sopranos. Brightly coloured slings have been fashionable, but the vivid colours can clash horribly with clothing. For the alto and larger saxophones it's possible to use the sling without adjusting the length each time you play. This has the advantage of enabling you to maintain a consistent posture and helps consistent embouchure formation.

CASES need to be strong and light. Soft bags have been in vogue, but offer only minimum protection for the saxophone. They are fine if you can be sure that your instrument is always transported by hand. A soft case is no protection at all if stowed beneath heavy gear. Shaped plastic (usually fibreglass) cases look very eye-catching, but fall over easily, and won't stow in much less space than a conventional case. Be careful when using your case as a storage place for music etc. It's very easy to strain the hinges. The saxophone case is often regarded as part of one's image, one's 'street credibility'. This is an understandable tendency but not very wise as a first priority.

It's false economy to buy a cheap or unreliable **Saxophone stand.** You will come to share this opinion once you have seen a good instrument bady damaged by falling from a poor stand. Beware of borrowed stands! Use the correct pegs for clarinet and flute.

Basic Techniques — Sound

EMBOUCHURE
Describes the formation of lips, teeth, cheeks and jaw muscles used to play a wind instrument. It's a French word, meaning mouthpiece or the opening of a bag or the mouth of a river!

Avoid puffing out your cheeks. It reduces your endurance and control, and spoils your good looks! Only when attempting *circular breathing* (blowing through your mouth while simultaneously breathing in through your nose) is it helpful to puff out your cheeks. Most saxophonists play with their top teeth in contact with the mouthpiece, finding that this gives more control and greater endurance than when the top lip comes between teeth and mouthpiece. Although the bottom lip acts as a cushion between teeth and reed DO NOT hold the bottom lip TIGHTLY folded back over your teeth.

You can approximate the feel of the lower lip position by using your first and second fingers to represent the mouthpiece. Put the two fingers into your mouth almost up to the middle joint, with top teeth resting on fingers, bottom lips folded back TIGHTLY over your teeth. Slowly pull your fingers out of your mouth by between half and three quarters of an inch, allowing the bottom lip to be pulled slightly outwards into a slight pout. Once you are used to this type of embouchure you'll find that it gives you a richer, freer, and more flexible sound than the tighter 'folded back' embouchure. If in any doubt consult a teacher or experienced player. Study action photographs of well-known saxophonists.

Developing your embouchure muscles is achieved in a manner similar to any other kind of muscular (athletic) training — by concentrated performance of the task in question. If you are to develop your embouchure muscles you will make best use of your time if you concentrate on this task *only.* By playing LONG NOTES you can focus your attention on sound production, and avoid being distracted by problems of reading, or the difficulties of getting your fingers around tricky passages. Long-note practice is also useful for studying your breath control, and perfecting your vibrato. If you are trying to improve the quality of your tone, then listen to a recording of the player you admire before you play. Get the sound into your 'mind's ear' so that your embouchure muscles can work towards recreating that sound. Long-note practice can be tiring to your embouchure, so apportion your work time sensibly. Of course you shouldn't play a lot of long notes if you have a lengthy performance to undertake later in the day. A good alternative to long-note practice is the playing of slow melodies. It's an alternative that is particularly appreciated by peace-loving neighbours!

Here are some typical long-note exercises. The ticks indicate breathing points:

Long-Note Exercises

(2)   ♩ = 120

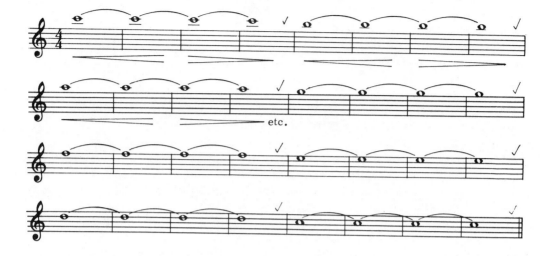

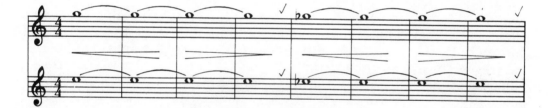

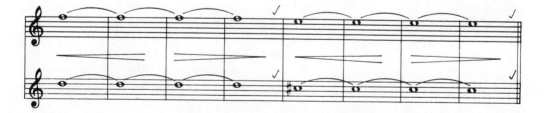

(3)   ♩ = 120

9

BREATHING: USING YOUR DIAPHRAGM

Rest your fingertips at the top of your stomach just below your ribs. Snatch a very quick deep breath without raising your shoulders. You'll feel your stomach push out. The diaphragm is the muscle at the bottom of the lungs, above the stomach, and deep breathing requires that you use the diaphragm and can feel the top of your abdomen move outwards to accommodate the air. You'll find that many problems of saxophone playing are considerably reduced if you remember to breathe from the diaphragm and thus support the notes with plenty of air. **This does not mean that you play louder or that you blow harder.**

Think of the sound quality for which you are striving before you begin the exercises. Try to imitate a few notes from an especially good recorded example by an admired player. Remind yourself by playing a few bars of a recording before you begin. Aim to keep the pitch steady, independent of the changes in volume. (Changes in volume are known as changes in *dynamics*). Ask your teacher or a friendly experienced player to play the following exercise with you, as a duet. If you tune up very carefully before you begin, and play accurately, you'll hear a third note generated between you. This *difference tone* is caused by the difference in frequency between the two saxophones. Once you have spotted the difference tone notice how sensitive it is to any slight change in pitch by one of the saxophones.

TONE

Imagine a simple melody played by your favourite saxophonist. Even when playing a simple tune, your performance, and the imagined performance by your favourite player, will be quite different. The main reason for the difference will be because you each have your own personal tone quality. When playing a simple melody the major personal contribution you make is your own (beautiful) tone. Of course tone characteristics are influenced by choice of reed, mouthpiece and instrument, by your tuning, the vibrato you employ, and the volume at which you play. Although these factors modify your tone considerably, the greatest determinant of tone quality is YOU — the many muscles of your lips and face which form the embouchure, together with the muscles of your throat, chest and diaphragm. Rather like an accent in your speech, your tone is largely 'caught' from what you hear around you. It is acquired by a process of imitation, influencing your muscles to seek the sound you have in your imagination. To acquire a particular type of tone:

1) Play along with recordings of your favourite player.
2) Hear live performances of your favourite player.
3) When choosing a teacher make his tone one of the important considerations.
4) Concentrate on the quality of sound when playing simple melodies.

Revise the scales of F major, D minor melodic and D minor harmonic.

OPEN THROAT

Away from the saxophone try to simulate the effect of a yawn, but without opening your mouth. This has the effect of *opening* your throat. Now try playing the saxophone with an open throat. You'll find that it alters the tone quality, having a particularly good effect on the lower part of the instrument and on the lower saxophones.

On the saxophone there are three fingerings for each Bb:

In **Burindi,** however, the most suitable is the fingering for the **A,** one semitone below, plus the lower right hand side key operated by the side of the right hand index finger. You will find further discussion and supplementary material for practice of Bb fingerings on page 14.

Make sure you play all the long notes to their full value:

(End on <u>three</u>.)

Burindi

SLOW MELODIES

The simple long note exercises on pages 8–10 are designed to allow you to concentrate on the quality of the sound you make. But long note exercises can become very boring, and you can introduce variety into your practice by playing slow melodies. Broadway show tunes make good material. Search through song books for suitable examples. Try BLUE JOHN by a lesser-known writer to get you started!

Blue John

Revise the scales of Bb major, G minor melodic and G minor harmonic.

Next, another slow melody but this time containing quarter note triplets ($\lceil\overset{3}{\quad}\rceil$). Play the triplets smoothly, with each note of equal value. If this is difficult think of the music as having an underlying pulse of two in a bar. For practice away from the saxophone, try saying the word 'lazily' to yourself in the time of two beats whilst tapping or counting a steady four. Make each syllable of equal length, of course!

An alternative fingering for Bb is to use the left hand index finger *only* to cover the button for B *and* the small button between B and A. Try holding down both buttons with one finger. This fingering is particularly useful for figures on the diminished arpeggio which includes Bb. Play the following exercises several times, using this new Bb fingering. Play slowly and rhythmically, and gradually increase the tempo.

(1)

(2)

The small button between B and A is called the *bis* key. Although the side B♭ fingering discussed on page 11 can be used in most circumstances, some players use the *bis* fingering more than other B♭ fingerings. It certainly avoids the problem of co-ordination between right and left hand, but has the disadvantage that alternating between B and B♭ is difficult. Try it.

In **Aswan,** once again, give the notes their exact duration.

(off on *four*)

Continue to count or tap an even four during the one bar rest. This is essential when you play with others, so establish the habit *now*.
Notice the difference between a whole note rest and a half note rest:

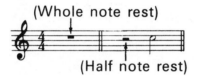

(Whole note rest)

(Half note rest)

If you know the notes by their English names you can remember which rest is which by saying:

<u>M</u>inims <u>M</u>ounted
<u>S</u>emibreves <u>S</u>uspended

The whole note rest is also used as the symbol for *any* silent bar, for example:

For this reason, the whole note rest is not normally used for less than one bar.

Aswan

Revised the scales of Eb major, C minor melodic and C minor harmonic.

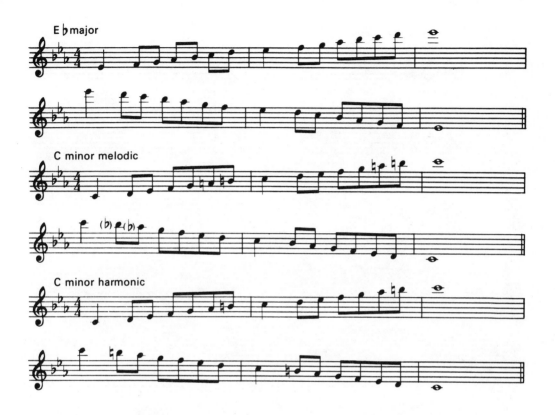

Try the following duet with a friend.

E♭ Duet

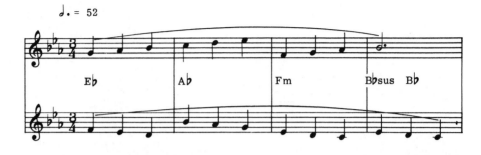

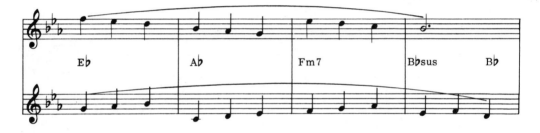

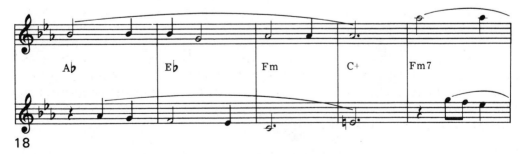

18

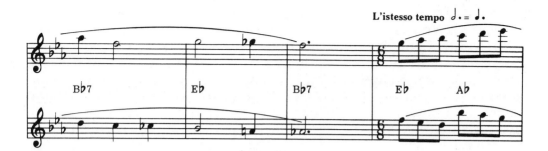

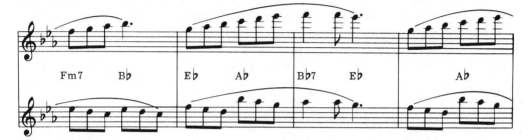

L'istesso tempo means 'the same speed'. Although the notation changes, the speed of performance of the melody remains the same.

VIBRATO

Vibrato is frequently a contentious subject. One often hears the argument 'John Coltrane (or Charlie Parker, Phil Woods, Mike Brecker, or some other admired player) didn't use vibrato'. This is simply not true, and betrays unobservant listening. All four great jazz players *did* use vibrato. Classical saxophonists use vibrato. Almost all styles of saxophone music call for vibrato at some time. Skilful use of vibrato prevents it from being obtrusive or distracting. What *can* be distracting when you first hear vibrato correctly done in performance is that the effect must be slightly exaggerated on the platform if it is to sound correct to an audience seated at some distance. The same reduction in effect also occurs in recordings and broadcasts, and compensating for this vibrato loss is part of the art of microphone technique gained by observation and experience.

Saxophone vibrato is best achieved by a slight up and down jaw movement. You can approximate the jaw action by saying WAH-WAH-WAH-WAH. To begin with make the vibrato by lowering the pitch of the note and returning. Achieve this by a *very slight* slackening of the jaw. Make the pulses slow at first. For most saxophonists the muscular action to achieve vibrato *feels* as though the pitch is being lowered and returned, although the evidence of the electronic tuner suggests an even distribution either side of the note. At first, allow the note to become established before adding vibrato. Some styles of playing call for 'instant vibrato' however. Experiment with the speed and depth of vibrato. Try making the vibrato pulses in multiples of the tempo of the music. Vibrato sounds better if you make it slightly faster for higher notes, slower for very low ones. Above all, listen to the vibrato of other saxophonists, and other instrumentalists and singers. Analyse what they are doing. Notice how certain tone qualities are linked to a particular vibrato. An excellent chapter on vibrato can be found in Weisberg's *The Art of Wind Playing*.[5]

Return to the long-note exercises on page 8 and play them again, this time using vibrato. Repeat some of the slow tunes, adding vibrato to the longer notes. **The Old Castle** is another slow melody — a famous orchestral solo, with vibrato, but first revise the scales of A♭ major, F minor melodic and F minor harmonid.

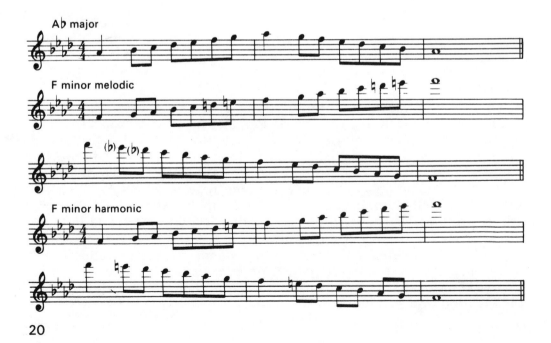

The Old Castle

MOUSSORGSKY (1839-1881)

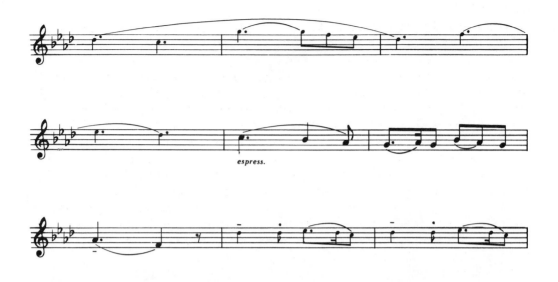

The small note (*) with a line through the stem is called an acciaccatura (ak-ee-ak-a-chur-a), literally a 'crushing' note. The acciaccatura is, strictly, an ornament used only in keyboard music prior to the mid-eighteenth century, where it is struck *on* the beat together with the note it adorns. In saxophone music you can imitate the keyboard effect by playing the *inessential* note on the beat and moving very quickly to the *essential* note.

MOUTHPIECES

Choose a mouthpiece to suit *you*, not because someone else has that model. Nevertheless, take note of fashion and what others are using, and find out why. When trying a mouthpiece play it in several acoustic environments, and above all *try it when playing in an ensemble*. Give yourself time to get accustomed to the mouthpiece, and choose a reed to suit — though for quick comparative purposes using your well-played reed and your own instrument reduces the number of variables. Make sure you re-tune when choosing between several mouthpieces, for playing the instrument off-pitch can induce unconscious embouchure adjustments which hinder comparison. No mouthpiece will give good intonation when the tuning is far away from concert pitch. You can gain useful insight into the characteristics of mouthpieces by loading the inside of your mouthpiece with chewing gum or modelling clay. More controlled experiments can be conducted by melting wax onto the inside of the mouthpiece and carefully sculpting it.

Revise the scales of D♭ major, B♭ minor melodic and B♭ minor harmonic.

Here is another famous orchestral saxophone solo. Use a little vibrato on notes longer than an eighth note.

L'Arlesienne, Suite 1   BIZET (1838-1875)

ALTO SAX SOLO *from* **CARILLON**

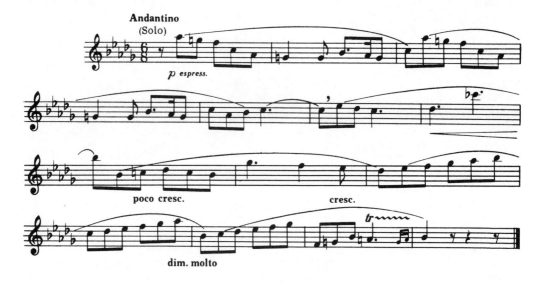

A trill or shake (tr〰〰) is a rapid alternation of the written note and the note above. The trill ends in a turn *below* the written note. In the Bizet example the trill is written out. In earlier music (well before the invention of the saxophone) the convention was that it began on the note *above* the written note.

REEDS

Cane reeds are made up from an enormous number of tiny tubes. Take a new unblown cane reed. Thoroughly soak it in water and with water lying on the blade (the cut portion) blow hard *through* the reed from butt to tip. Many bubbles of air will be seen fizzing of 'frying' on the cut surface of the reed. This demonstrates the existence of the tubes and the free passage of air through these tubes. Now do the same with a well-used reed. Apart from noticing that water will not lie as easily on a used reed you'll find that the air doesn't pass through the reed. A well-used reed has the tubes obstructed in some way. This may be due to saliva-borne detritus entering the reed, or the action of embouchure and tongue may have crushed the tubes.

You can prolong the life of a reed, and speed up the blowing-in process by carefully stroking the blade of a new reed with a smooth hard object. This crushes the ends of the tiny tubes, obstructing entry to the body of the reed and slightly reducing its resistance. Make a few smoothing movements, *wet* the blade of the reed and blow through the butt of the reed again. Fewer bubbles will appear. Repeat until the flow of bubbles has been substantially reduced. A reed that has undergone this simple preparation will offer slightly less resistance and have a longer life. (Obviously you can't carry out this preparation with a plastic coated reed). You'll probably notice that softer reeds play flatter than hard reeds. When changing to a different strength reed you'll need to re-tune.

REED SQUEAKS

A reed squeak is an ugly distraction, and worth making some effort to avoid. The problem may be the fault of the instrument, tuning, mouthpiece or reed — or a combination of these. Attempt to isolate the cause by elimination. The following list will help you discover the cause of the squeak.

AREA	CAUSE
Instrument	Leaking instrument. Octave mechanism out of adjustment. Obstruction lodged in bore (e.g. mouthpiece cap).
Tuning	Saxophone flat to accompanying instruments or one note may be badly out of tune, due to instrument maladjustment. Exaggerated embouchure compensation may cause squeak. A very tight embouchure can promote squeaks. For proof, gently bite the reed with your bottom teeth.
Mouthpiece	Very bright, edgy sounding mouthpieces are most likely to squeak. Very narrow or damaged tip rail increases likelihood of squeaks. Any distortion or asymmetry may cause squeaks. Check the symmetry of the lay of the side rails by inserting a card behind the reed. Both side rails should touch the reed at the same distance from the tip. If they don't the card will come to rest at a lop-sided angle.
Reed	Unbalanced reed. One side of the reed offers much greater resistance then the other. This is a very common cause of squeaks.

You can compare the resistance of each side of the reed by taking the assembled reed mouthpiece and crook, and trapping one edge of the reed along one side rail with one side of your mouth. The mouthpiece will have to enter your mouth at an extreme sideways angle. Blow so that only half of the reed vibrates. Repeat the process for the other half of the reed. For most reeds, you'll find that one side of the reed vibrates more freely than the other. Using a sharp blade scrape the stiffer side gently until both sides of the reed offer the same resistance to blowing. This will considerably reduce the likelihood of squeaks.

TRIMMING THE REED TIP

If the reed is marginally too soft, or has developed a jagged tip, you can use a reed cutter to trim the end of the reed. This is a small specially-designed guillotine, shaped exactly to fit the tip of a particular size of reed. (When buying one you'll need to specify whether you require the cutter for a soprano, alto, tenor or baritone saxophone). Before you purchase it, try the cutter on a reed in the shop. You'll need to take your mouthpiece with you because very occasionally the cut is not symmetrical, and the trimmed reed won't be an exact fit on the mouthpiece.

In the absence of a reed cutter a useful improvised method for trimming a reed is to 'burn it back'. This works well with a metal mouthpiece but don't try it if your mouthpiece is plastic or rubber until you are skilled at the technique. Experiment first on an old reed and mouthpiece. Extend the reed very slightly beyond the tip rail of the mouthpiece.

Choose a coin with a radius to match the curve of the mouthpiece tip rail. Trap the reed between the mouthpiece and the coin, with approximately 1 mm protruding and with a flame (a match or a cigarette lighter) burn away the protruding tip of the reed, working very carefully to obtain a smooth radius.

Basic Techniques — Tonguing

To achieve a clean and fast tonguing technique use only the front portion of the tongue.

Check that only the front portion of the tongue moves, and that you don't move jaw or embouchure muscles. Any movement more than that which is absolutely necessary is bound to reduce efficiency.

Breathing from the diaphragm is essential. A good supply of air is required to make the note sound when the tongue releases the reed. When difficulties arise, they are more frequently because of poor co-ordination between tongue and fingers, than being unable to tongue quickly. The co-ordination study on page 32 demonstrates this. The speed at which your tongue has to move is quite moderate, but it must act in exact co-ordination with your fingers. Here again, you'll find that having good breath support is a help.

Speed of tonguing is also affected by the strength of the reed, the lay of the mouthpiece, and the way you place the reed in relation to the mouthpiece. Experiment!

DOUBLE TONGUING can be achieved by moving the tongue up and down across the end of the mouthpiece, tonguing one note on the up movement and the next on the down movement. (Used by orchestral clarinettists). It's difficult at first, but effective when mastered, and can be co-ordinated with changes of fingering.

FLUTTER TONGUING is used as an expressive device rather than as a means of starting a note. Flutter your tongue as though rolling R's.

VERY FAST TONGUING can be done by moving your tongue horizontally across the reed just below the tip. This can be executed so quickly that it's impossible to co-ordinate with a change of note, so is most effective on one note. It's very hard on the tongue, so 'little and often' is the way to attempt this.

SLAP TONGUE. Long before you took up the saxophone you could probably make a smacking noise in your mouth by sucking a vacuum between your tongue and the the roof of your mouth, and suddenly withdrawing your tongue. Substitute the reed for the pallet of your mouth and start a note by making this smacking effect which is difficult, but most effective on very low notes. Use the centre of your tongue, not the tip.

Revise the scales of C major, A minor melodic and A minor harmonic and then try *L'Arlesienne.*

L'Arlesienne, Suite 1

BIZET

ALTO SAX SOLO *from* **OVERTURE**

A third fingering for B♭ (or, later, as in the first bars of **Bink's Waltz**, A♯) is to play B♮ and add the middle finger of the right hand.

In flat keys, however, it's more logical to use the first finger of the right hand rather than the middle finger. This is useful in rapid shifts from F to B♭ in arpeggio figures. It's ideal for instance, in the first complete bar of the following hornpipe. From the three fingerings you now know, choose the most suitable fingering for the B♭ in the final three bars.

Hornpipe

Revise the scales of G major, E minor melodic and E minor harmonic.

In **Bink's Waltz** use B♭ fingering for the phrase:

Tongue the third bar gently. No emphasis is needed, just sufficient attack to sound each reiterated note. The *staccato* eighth notes in the fifth bar are given more emphasis of course. For further practice at gentle *legato* tonguing, revise **Blue John** on page 13.

The signs relating to note lengths are usually limited to the following, in order of duration. (There is an increase in volume but also in brevity down the list).

Tenuto

Staccato

Marcato

Superlative marcato

Bink's Waltz

SCOTT JOPLIN (1868-1917)

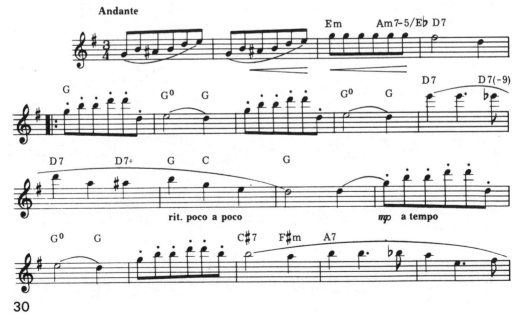

30

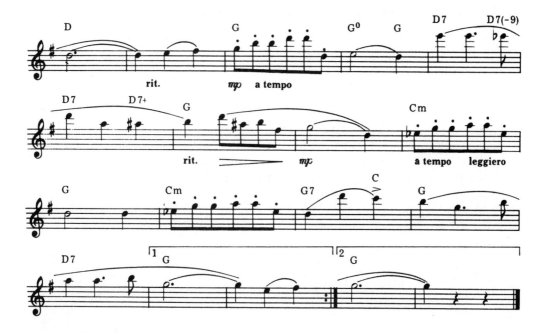

Revise the scales of D major, B minor melodic and B minor harmonic.

CO-ORDINATION STUDY — TONGUE AND FINGERS

Play strictly in time. Start slowly (around ♩ = 60) and only increase the speed when you can play the piece cleanly and accurately.

Revise the scales of A major, F♯ minor melodic and F♯ minor harmonic.

Three Irish Jigs

These are exercises for tonguing reiterated notes. First tongue every note, then experiment with different articulations.

1. THE TENPENNY BIT

2. THE IRISH WASHERWOMAN

Revise the scales of E major, C♯ minor melodic and C♯ minor harmonic.

3. ST. PATRICK'S DAY

Revise the scales of B major, G♯ minor melodic and G♯ minor harmonic.

B major

G♯ minor melodic

*Ossia

G♯ minor harmonic

*Ossia means *or*

Fairy Dance (Eightsome Reel)

Revise the scale of F♯ major (G♭ major), E♭ minor melodic and E♭ minor harmonic.

D♯ minor (the relative minor to F♯) is so seldom used it is not included here.

The De'il Among the Tailors

From the ninth bar onwards, use the *bis* fingering for **A#** where this is part of an arpeggio figure.

The sharp key signatures in the last five exercises are simply the alto saxophone transpositions from the keys in which these pieces are usually played, in the violin-dominated traditional Scottish dance bands.

THE USE OF THE TONGUE IN JAZZ

Many styles of improvisation are inextricably linked with the way that notes are articulated — particularly in the way in which strings of 'rolled' eighth notes are tongued. This is a major aspect of the study of jazz styles, usually grasped intuitively rather than consciously studied, and best approached by careful listening, transcription (see page 62), and the guidance of a good teacher. To get an impression of the difference that tonguing can make to a passage, practise these four ways of playing the same phrase in D minor. In all cases the tonguing should be soft but precise. The exercise is concerned with the use of the tongue only. The next chapter is written to help you with playing the eighth notes in a jazz style.

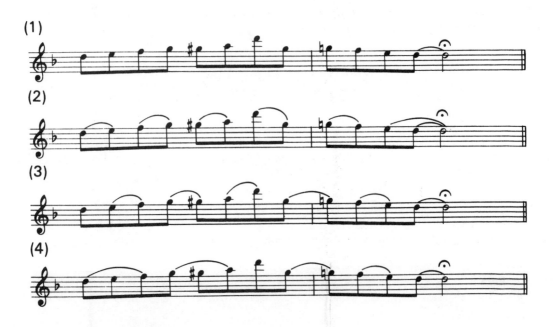

Jazz-based styles of playing

Play the following passage carefully:

If you played the time values of the notes correctly, the pairs of dotted eighth and sixteenth notes (quavers and semiquavers) were in the ratio 3:1.

In Jazz and Swing styles, however, dotted eighth notes and sixteenth notes are usually played in the ratio 2:1.

38

For music originally in four-four time the correct effect is gained if music is rewritten in twelve-eight:

Of course it's not practical to re-write the music in this way. The performer is expected to interpret the music in an appropriate style.

Practise playing the dotted eighth notes and sixteenth notes in the ratio 2:1 in the following four bar passage, written as a brief preparatory study for the duet DO IT YOURSELF.

Usually in jazz styles the dots and flags are omitted for clarity and ease of writing. Only when *even* quavers are required is an instruction given — usually the word 'even', or the addition of tenuto marks:

In all ensemble playing, pay attention to the duration of notes that are followed by rests. (In the last bar of the above example, the half note C comes off on the third beat). In worrying about what's coming next it's easy to be innaccurate about the ends of long notes. Giving long notes less than their correct duration is a very common fault.

Do It Yourself

Gently Swinging ♩ = 112

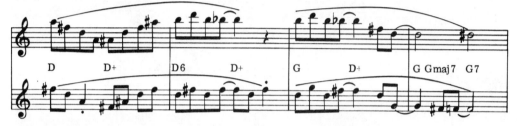

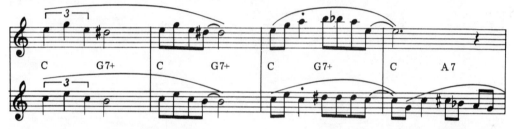

Hoagy

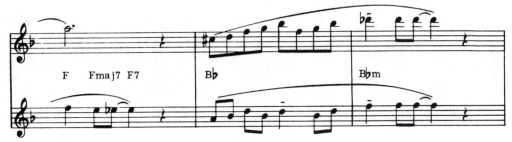

A7

Dm

G7

D.C. al

C

C7

F7   D♭7 C7

p

F

G7   C7

F

43

Look again at the duet **Hoagy,** at the penultimate bar before the return to the beginning. The notes across the beat have *marcato* accents (>). One of the general tendencies in jazz-based styles — it's almost a rule — is that *quarter notes across the beat are played short,* unless marked otherwise of course.

The bar written like this:

may also be written like this:

or this:

. . . . and the same effect obtained. The third of these alternatives is not recommended, however, because it offends a very sensible rule of musical notation which states that *in common time the centre of the bar should be seen.* If you were wondering why example one was much easier to read than example three, this is the reason. Avoid placing a quarter note across the middle of a bar of four-four. Join two eighth notes instead — it's much easier to read. Marcato accents are written above the notes that cross the beat in 'Hoagy', but in much of the music you will encounter, the accents will be omitted. You'll be expected to interpret the short notes for yourself.

Whistlin' in the Dark has no accents, but has many quarter notes across the beat. Play them short. They should come out shorter than the eighth notes that surround them. *Don't* forget to play the dotted eighth notes in the manner already outlined, and *do* give the full duration to half notes (and dotted half notes) when they are followed by a rest.

44

Whistlin' in the Dark

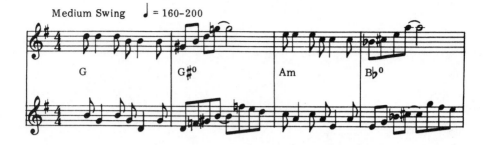

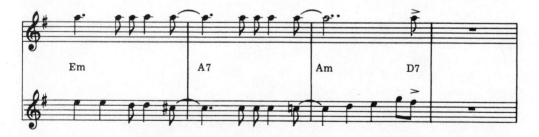

quick turn!

Notice the double-dotted note in bar fifteen. *Two dots placed after a note increase its value by three quarters.*

In this instance, the notes in the bottom part of the duet give you the exact position of the final eighth note in the top part.

IMPROVING YOUR SIGHT-READING

Include sight-reading as part of your daily routine. Don't try to sight-read major concert works that really require long and thoughtful study; that's a waste of time. Such pieces are not meant to be skimmed through, and you are quite likely to get a distorted image of the work if you don't prepare it carefully from the beginning. Instead, make a special collection of sight-reading material. Collect not-too-difficult rhythmic music approximating to that which a working saxophonist would be expected to read at sight. Always choose a tempo at which you can manage the most difficult bars. Play in time throughout, don't stop, and don't go back until you've finished the piece. Try to keep a smooth uninterrupted flow of music. Wrong notes are always preferable to stopping and starting. After all, you can't choose when to stop and start when sight-reading in an ensemble. Develop the habit of keeping going. Duets are superb for sight-reading practice, especially if your partner is a better reader then you. Seize every opportunity for ensemble playing, even if you hate the music! A professional is very fortunate if he only plays what pleases him.

In developing sight-reading, it's helpful to examine the skills of a person who can read literature aloud at sight in a fluent logical manner. He has a sense of the logic of the piece he's reading — he's telling a story, giving you more than mere words. He also needs to avoid stumbling or hesitation, and to do these things he needs to read at a *comfortable speed* and to *read ahead* of the words he's actually pronouncing. He must not stop or go back.

When reading music you can develop the trick of reading ahead by asking your teacher (or a friend who can read music) to hold a small piece of card over the music as you play, covering up the actual bar you are playing, and moving forward in time with your performance. This will force you to read ahead.

Rhythms in a rock-based style are known also as jazz-rock, jazz-funk and eight-eight style. When playing in the older jazz styles in four-four time, the rhythms are based on an underlying pulse of two and four. By contrast, in more recent rock-influenced music there is an even eighth note pulse present. As you've already seen, in jazz styles eighth and quarter notes are not always given their exact durations, but are interpreted. In rock styles, note values tend to be played as seen. Thus, the passage at bar thirteen of the next piece, **Khamsin** . . . .

.... will still have the dotted eighth notes and sixteenth notes played in the ratio 3:1.

Notice the sign for a *fall* in the above example, and in bar two:

The *fall* may be chromatic or diatonic. The latter is easier in this example. The end of the fall should be indeterminate; the listener should not hear a specific final note. Some players observe a rule that says: *'fall' for the duration of the written note.* Unfortunately this maxim is not universally observed. If you *can* persuade other players in your combo to abide by the convention however, you will achieve neater ensemble playing.

The opening notes of Khamsin can be played with two sets of fingerings:

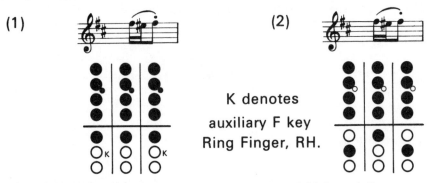

K denotes
auxiliary F key
Ring Finger, RH.

The fingering given in (2) is recommended here. For most purposes most players would use the second fingerings. The use of the first fingering given — first finger RH plus the ring finger RH on the auxiliary F key — is to be used:

1. For trills, F to F.
2. For moving between F and F when a very smooth transition between the notes is required, e.g. when playing a quiet but conspicuous solo.
3. In chromatic scales.

Experiment with these fingerings when moving from E to F in THE DE'IL AMONG THE TAILORS on page 37.

Khamsin

49

IDIOMATIC NOTATION

Dip

An embouchure and (maybe) fingering-assisted lowering and return of pitch, of at least a semitone. Usually drawn like a cartoonist's seagull, though sometimes the lines are drawn straight.

Doink

A rise in pitch, chromatically fingered or with embouchure and fingers, ending in a fade at an indeterminate higher pitch. Used most often in band ensembles. Doink, is of course, onomatopoeic.

Fall *or* Spill

A downward glissando, lip or finger-assisted lip, ending in a diminuendo at an indefinite pitch. There is a much-flouted convention that the fall lasts only for the duration of the written note. It should not encroach on the following note.

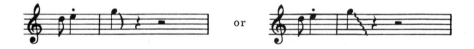

Glissando *('gliss')*

Sliding between two notes, done with the keys.

When performed with the lips or embouchure, it's called a *lip gliss,* or *lip slur.*

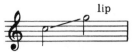

Ghosted Note
A note played so quietly that the pitch is difficult to identify. That note is then given in brackets.

Sometimes the note head is made into a cross.

It is preferable to decide the pitch of a ghosted note and notate in the bracket.

Growl
A dirtying of the tone achieved by growling in the throat.

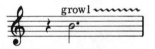

Lip Up *or* Scoop
A short lip-controlled portamento from below the note.

Melodic Curve
When there is a rapid agglomeration of notes played in a rubato flurry, conventional notation may be inadequate. The contour of the melody is all that can be given.

Patterns — Time Savers

SCALES AND ARPEGGIOS

Scales and arpeggios should form a proportion of your regular practice time. They are important technique builders, and whatever your aims regarding the saxophone you will need technique. In these next pages an attempt is made to show how to make your practice of these rudiments more interesting, more efficient, and more challenging by grouping each into one all-embracing pattern. Basing these patterns on a harmonic scheme, this also makes a good introduction to improvisation. This is not to suggest that you use the exercises as 'licks', but as a means of discovering your instrument from a harmonic viewpoint.

Symbols are used to indicate the harmonic scheme on which the patterns in this chapter are based. For the present, only four types of chord use used:

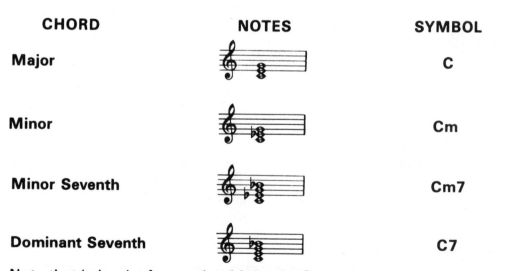

CHORD	NOTES	SYMBOL
Major		C
Minor		Cm
Minor Seventh		Cm7
Dominant Seventh		C7

Note that 'minor' refers to the third only. Sevenths are always a *minor seventh* above the root unless indicated otherwise.

You'll understand the following patterns better if you work them out for yourself. For this reason each one is left unfinished.

Patterns based on major triads

7.

E A D G C F

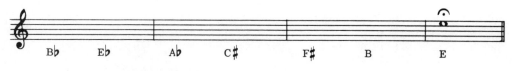

Bb Eb Ab C# F# B E

8.

A D G C

F Bb Eb Ab

Db F# B E A

9.

C Db D Eb

E F Gb G Ab

A Bb B C G7 C

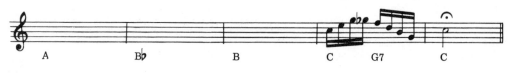

Patterns based on minor triads

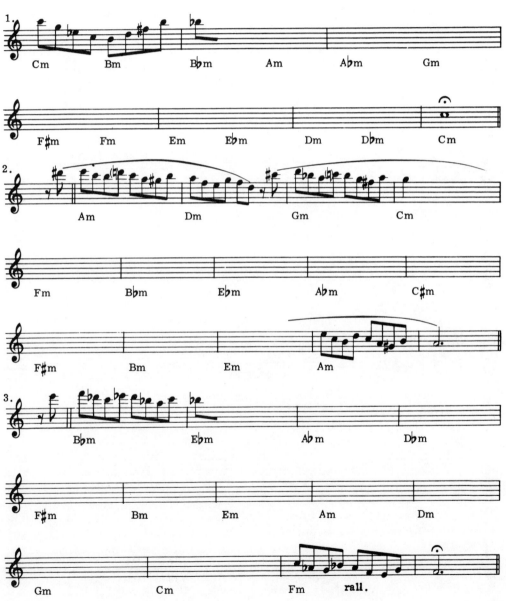

Dominant Seventh Patterns

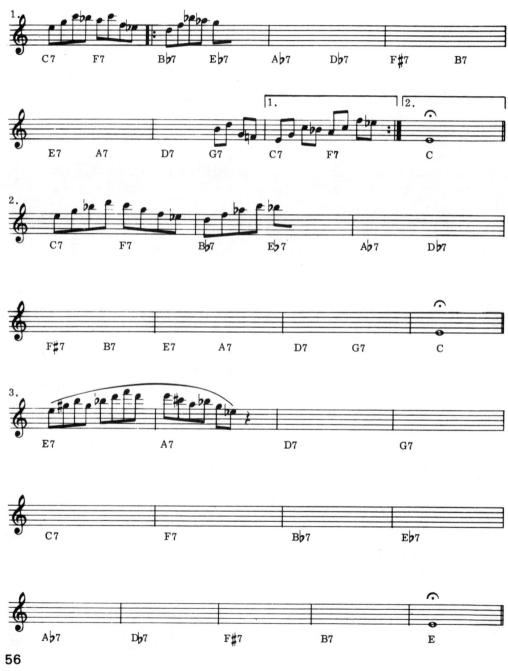

Minor Seventh and Dominant Seventh Combined

1.
Em7   A7   D   Dm7   G7   C   Cm7   F7   Bb

Bbm7   Eb7   Ab   Abm7   Db7   Gb   F#m7   B7   E

2.
Am7   D7   G   Cm7   F7   Bb

Ebm7   Ab7   Db   F#m7   B7   E

3.
Em7   A7   D   Gm7   C7   F

Bbm7   Eb7   Ab   C#m7   F#7   B

4.
Am7   D7   G   Cm7   F7   Bb

Ebm7   Ab7   Db   F#m7   B7   E

5.
Em7   A7   D   Gm7   C7   F

Bbm7   Eb7   Ab   Dbm   Gb7(F#7)   B

THE DIMINISHED SCALE
This is a nine note scale, in steps of semitone and tone alternating.

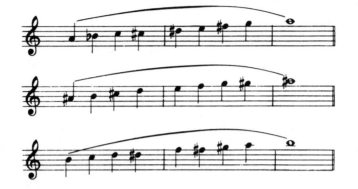

If this scale is played over a dominant seventh chord built on the first, third, fifth or seventh degrees of the scale, some of the colourful higher extensions of the chord are automatically introduced:

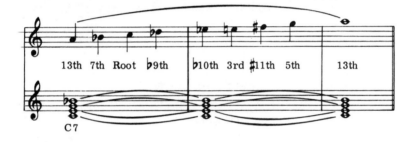

Exercises on the diminished scales

These are just a few patterns to get you started. Try to discover your own. There are numerous possibilities, and it will be easier to investigate them if you have some understanding of harmony. You'll find many more patterns in the following:

Thesaurus of Scales and Melodic Patterns Slonimsky, N. Duckworth and Co. London 1975.

Patterns for Improvisation Nelson, O. Noslen Music Co. Los Angeles 1966.

Jazz Improvisation Kynaston, T.P. and Ricci, R.J. Spectrum Books. Prentice Hall Inc., 1978.

Patterns for Jazz Coker, J., Casale, J., Campbell, G., Greene, J. Studio Publications, Lebanon Indiana. 1970.

THE DO'S AND DONT'S OF PRACTICE
DO develop a routine:
1) Always check that you are tuned to concert pitch.
2) Try to memorise something every day.
3) Keep a check on what you are doing. Carry a pencil in your saxophone case and note the tempo at which you can play that tricky passage accurately. Subdivide those difficult rhythms with feint pencil 'slash marks' so that you don't have to start from scratch again tomorrow.

DON'T start by choosing a new reed. Practise first. Otherwise the 'reed seeking' will follow Parkinson's Law, and fill the time available.

DO save lip-taxing items (high note harmonics, etc.) until last.

DON'T give a performance for those within earshot. If you find that you are tempted to waste your practice time in this way, try to find a more private place to work.

DO isolate problem passages and work economically at just those bits. Don't take an eight-bar run up each time.

DON'T play your showy bits and pieces unnecessarily — licks, concerto high spots, favourite solos. Work at what you can't do, not what you can do.

MASSED PRACTICE VERSUS DISTRIBUTED PRACTICE

There is evidence that the human body continues to work on the process of learning even when we seem to be uninvolved with the subject we are studying, maybe when we are at rest or at play. When we are not actively learning (practising), our body subconsciously sifts, organises and generally makes sense of the material we have been studying. To some extent this explains why a much-practised difficult passage often seems to be easier to play when we return to it after a break of hours or days. It also means that difficult music is more efficiently tackled if it is practised over a period, in well-distributed work sessions, rather than attempted in one marathon session. Therefore, *providing the practice periods are long enough to be effective,* it is better to spread your practice over several sessions. Three one-hour sessions are better than one three-hour session, for example.

It also means that, for the same time spent, you will learn more efficiently if you study over a period, rather than 'cramming' at the last minute.

Improvisation

Some skill in improvising is almost obligatory for most working saxophonists. Some players approach improvising in an analytical way, studying their material carefully. While their performances can/may be exciting and spontaneous, they are nevertheless executed from a standpoint of considerable knowledge and understanding. Others work largely by ear, finding their way through the accompanying chords by choosing notes that appeal to their own taste. They may do their practice by playing along with gramophone records. Particularly useful for this method are the specially produced records of a rhythm section playing the accompaniment for improvising. If you prefer a more analytical approach to the subject it's very helpful to read widely about improvising, and to make your first attempts by writing yourself a solo on a given chord progression. This will:

1. Help you to compose your own phrases.
2. Provide a record of your progress and achievements.
3. Help you to understand and memorise the chord progression (Don't call progressions 'sequences'. They are not necessarily the same thing, a sequence being a repetition of a pattern at a higher or lower level.)
4. Give you something to fall back on when spontaneous inspiration flags.

Try not to make the common mistake of giving yourself an enormous technical challenge in the solos you write. Start simply, choosing tunes that have few changes in harmony.

Here are two simple chord progressions on which you can experiment with some improvisation. One is a standard 32-bar A-B-A-C form popular song progression, and the other a variation on the traditional twelve-bar blues.

If you are new to improvisation you can begin by playing chord notes only, in tempo, to give you an idea of the direction in which the chords move:

Once you have an idea of the harmonic scheme you can add some non-chord notes:

Vary the harmonic tension by using non-chord notes to suit your own taste.

Chord Progressions

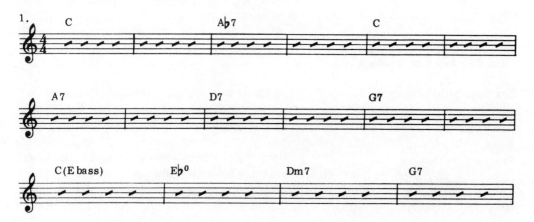

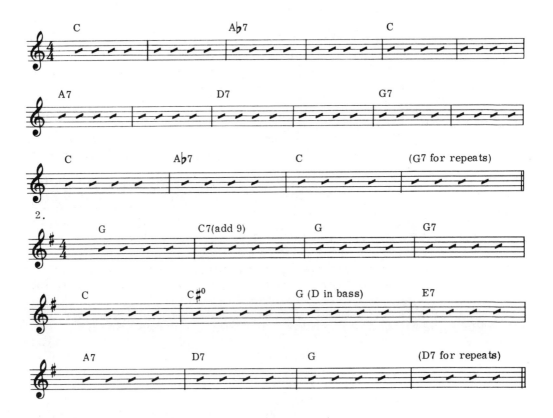

The Piano

Some ability at the keyboard is a great asset to the player of any instrument. The harmonic knowledge and understanding acquired is of great benefit if you are an aspiring jazz player. If you don't play the piano, do give some serious thought to the possibility of learning. It certainly won't harm your saxophone playing!

Transcription

So far only the rudimentary mechanics of improvisation have been discussed. Style has not been mentioned. Doubtless you will already have some ideas about the style towards which you are aiming. To heighten your awareness of the components of a particular style some concentrated listening is required. The most concentrated form of listening is *transcription,* the process of accurately writing down (and subsequently learning to play) an admired improvised solo. The easiest way to transcribe a recorded solo is to transfer the recording on to quarter inch tape and write out the solo note by note, either by using your aural ability or by playing along with the solo a few notes at a time. Using your instrument is preferable if you are trying to acquire the details of the performer's style. For difficult passages:

1. Have a rest and return fresh.
2. Continue at the next easy passage; it could be that the troublesome passage is repeated later in the piece and it may then be more clearly audible.
3. Try different playback speeds, or mono or single channel playback. Bass parts are easier to hear if they are played back at double speed. To do this you'll need a reel-to-reel machine; hence the suggestion (above) to transfer the recording on to quarter inch tape.
4. Ask another musician for his opinion.
5. Use your harmonic knowledge to guide you, remembering that some of the world's greatest players sometimes produce a 'wrong' note.
6. Use your knowledge of your instrument to decide which of the possibilities is most idiomatic.

Once the melody notes of the transcription are complete, check them by playing along on your instrument, maybe in octaves at half speed. At this point phrasing, dynamics, slurs and accents can be added. As most improvisation is relative to some background harmony the transcription of the melodic line only gives half the story, and is of little use for analytical purposes unless the harmonies are added. For jazz and rock performances of an improvised or semi-improvised type this means adding chord symbols. Don't simply take the chords from a publisher's copy or a friend's chord book. There's little chance of that being an accurate representation of what's on the recording. Transcribe the bass line. In conjunction with the melody and a little musical sense this will provide more than a hint of what the chord symbols should be.

The greatest value in transcriptions lies in doing them for yourself, but ready-prepared transcriptions are helpful, particularly if you have access to the original recording to hear those aspects of style that cannot be conveyed on paper. See *Front Line Sax Solos*[6] for a collection of twenty tenor saxophone transcriptions in a variety of jazz styles.

Here's a solo recorded by one of the most influential tenor saxophonists of the mid-twentieth century, Sonny Rollins. It was recorded in 1957 in New York, and issued on the French Musidisc label, in the *Jazz Anthology* series. The record was called *Sonny Rollins — First Recordings 1957*, number 30 JA 5128. If you can obtain a copy of the record you will notice that the performer's subtle sense of time is beyond precise notation — unless one resorts to impossibly complicated rhythms.

Theme from Tchaikovsky's Pathetic Symphony

(IMPROVISATION BY SONNY ROLLINS)

(croak)

Advanced Techniques

DOUBLE DENSITIES

Lester Young was the first great saxophonist to draw attention to the possibility of using unorthodox fingerings to create different densities of sound on one note. In his improvisations, he would sometimes repeat one note using a different fingering on alternate repetitions, achieving a subtle saxophonic equivalent of the open and closed effect obtained by the use of plunger mutes on brass instruments:

where o = open
      + = closed

There are many other uses for these alternate fingerings. They can be used to improve intonation, smooth out difficult passages, and are excellent preparation for playing the high notes above top F. If you can achieve the majority of the alternatives given for double densities above the stave then you'll find the high harmonics much easier to attempt.

Overblow bottom B♭. (Finger bottom B♭ and add octave key). Strong, hoarse, sound. Slightly sharp.

1. Overblow bottom B. Strong, hoarse, sound, slightly sharp.
2. Finger bottom D and remove index finger left hand (B). Very sharp — adjust embouchure.

1. Overblow bottom C, finger bottom C and add octave key. Strong, hoarse, sound.
2. Use RH side alternate C (finger B and add centre RH key with side of right index finger). Very smooth. Difference almost undetectable.
    Pitch comparison good for both alternatives.

Overblow bottom C♯ — strong, hoarse, sound. Slightly sharp.

1. Finger conventional D and add palm D key. Cleaner, more open sound, very effective on older saxophones. Pitch comparison good.
2. Palm D only, in lower register. Slightly flat.

1. Aux. F only, in low register.
2. Open C♯ low register with RH side E only. Slightly flat.
3. Finger conventional middle D♯ and add palm D and D♯ keys. More open sound, but note is liable to crack.
4. Finger high D♯ without octave key. Flat.

1. Finger high F on palm keys only, without octave key.
2. Finger conventional E, adding LH little finger on bottom B key. Sounds unimpressive in practice room, but noticeably aids carrying power in a saxophone section.

Finger conventional F. Add bottom C key (RH little finger) and bottom B♭ key (LH little finger). Good choked effect. Takes a wide vibrato very well to achieve a shake effect. Sharp.

Finger conventional F♯, add bottom C key (RH little finger) and bottom B key (LH little finger). Good choked effect.

Overblow bottom C.

1. Overblow bottom C♯. Modern saxophones have a linked C♯ / G♯ mechanism, so that the low C♯ key with LH little finger can be held down for both notes. Needs coaxing with embouchure. Slightly flat.
2. Finger A and lower pitch by adding first two fingers RH. Sharp.

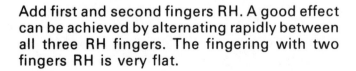

Add first and second fingers RH. A good effect can be achieved by alternating rapidly between all three RH fingers. The fingering with two fingers RH is very flat.

1. Finger A (a semitone below) and raise the pitch by adding all three fingers of RH plus E♭ key. Slightly veiled sound, but pitch is good. Useful both as an effect AND as another 'legitimate' fingering for fast movements between A and B♭.
2. Overblow bottom B♭. Skill with tongue and diaphragm needed to make note speak.

Overblow bottom B. Remarks as 2 above.

1. Overblow bottom C.
2. Use side key. (Finger B, add middle side key with RH index finger).

1. Overblow bottom C♯.
2. Overblow middle D but remove index finger LH.
3. Overblow middle F♯.
4. Overblow bottom D.

Overblow middle G. Maybe slightly sharp. If so, add bottom C key.

1. Overblow middle G♯. Sharp. Difficult to make note speak.
2. Finger top C♯ and add RH side key for E only. Sharp.

Finger top C♯ and add LH palm F only.

Overblow top A by opening palm D♯ slightly.

When trying these fingerings keep experimenting to seek better results. Keep a careful note of your discoveries.

High Note Fingering Chart

C

C♯

D

D♯

E

F

Palm D

Palm D and E♭

Palm D and E♭

Palm D and E♭

Overblow bottom B♭

Side E

Side C

Palm D, E♭ and F

Side E

Side C

Side E

E♭

Palm D and E♭

E♭

Decide on the most suitable fingerings for you. Mark them in the book and commit them to memory. At this stage don't try to memorize more than one fingering for each note.

High notes are very hard on your embouchure. Distribute your practice sessions and stop at the first signs of strain. When attempting the following high note arpeggio exercise build it up in small stages.

HIGH NOTE ARPEGGIO EXERCISES

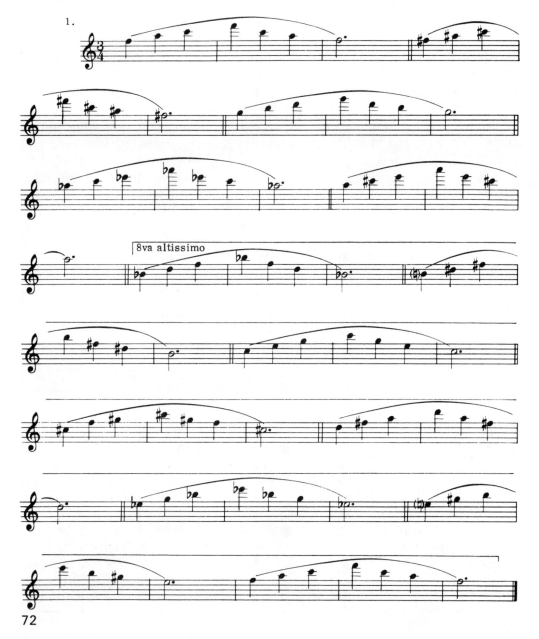

2. 8va altissimo throughout

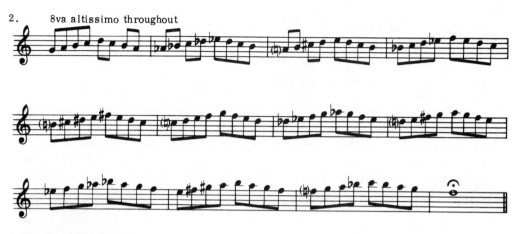

LIP GLISSANDO

The most famous single reed lip glissando is probably the clarinet entry at the beginning of Gershwin's *Rhapsody in Blue.* Amongst saxophone players the late Johnny Hodges used the lip glissando as a personal stylistic thumbprint.

Some players achieve a smooth glissando by maintaining a steady embouchure and gently sliding their fingers off the keys. This is difficult, and depends greatly on familiarity with one particular instrument. The upward *lip* glissando can only be achieved if you can first LOWER the pitch of a note in the upper register by at least a semitone. As a preparatory exercise play B:

. . . . and try lowering the pitch to A using your embouchure only.

Now play an A, and whilst changing the fingering to B, hold the pitch of the note down to A by slackening your embouchure so that the note rises very little or not at all. Now raise the pitch of the note towards B using your embouchure, breath and throat, whilst simultaneously fingering a still higher note — say C♯. The aim is to raise the pitch of the note by fingering, but always to be playing a note that is flat to the fingering you are using — until you reach the note you are aiming for. Smooth out the 'steps' of changing fingerings by using your embouchure. The whole process is extremely difficult to describe in writing. A demonstration from someone who can achieve a smooth lip glissando will be a great help.

Coda: What's New?

THE CONTEMPORARY SCENE

Popular music is ever-changing. The saxophone has been utilised in popular music for most of the twentieth century, and if you are wise you will make *some* attempt to keep up with new developments. Every generation of players seems to include some who latch on to a particularly well-loved specialism and refuse to move on even when there is less and less public demand for that style of playing. So beware! Of course you don't want to become an uncritical enthusiast for every new development, but it's prudent to try and evaluate each innovation as it appears. Try new mouthpieces, new makes of reeds, and play new models of saxophones. Listen out for the much-acclaimed new players and try to hear their records and attend their concerts. Investigate the other orchestral woodwind instruments, not forgetting the 'ethnic' wind such as the shakuhachi, the membrane flutes and the nai. Try some baroque wind instruments. Electronic developments should also be explored. Most of the effects now available to guitarists can now be available to the saxophonist by using a small specially designed microphone (a bug) attached to the mouthpiece.

Record shops, and the radio and television, are good sources of information about contemporary developments, but by using these sources you are always going to be hearing the 'new thing' after someone has used it. For really up-to-date information on what's new browse in good music shops for new instruments and new books. You should also read the better specialist music magazines. Particularly recommended are:

Down Beat, *222, West Adams Street, Chicago, IL 60606*
Long-standing American monthly, just about the best international magazine for jazz. Always carries a good selection of advertisements for music education material and 'play along' records. Much saxophone literature is advertised.

International Musician and Recording World, *141, Drury Lane, London WC2B 5TB.*
Good contemporary coverage. Has been known to review new models of saxophones when they appear.

Keyboard, *Subscription Dept. Box 28836, San Diego, CA 92128*
It may seem odd to recommend a keyboard magazine to a saxophonist, but this one does give very good coverage of all the latest electronic devices. Monthly.

Woodwind Brass and Percussion, *Evans Publications, 25 Court Street, Deposit, NY 13754*
Technical articles, music reviews. Good if you are interested in teaching. Published eight times a year.

Crescendo, *122 Wardour Street, London W1V 3LA*
Contains a regular 'Reed Clinic', and advertises specialist saxophone music. Monthly.

Jazz Journal, *4, Great Queen Street, London WC2B 5DG*
Reviews jazz records, festivals, concerts and some publications. Monthly.

Mixing with other enthusiasts is also a good way to know what's new. To this end you could consider joining the **Clarinet and Saxophone Society of Great Britain.** (Your local library will be able to supply the current address of the Society's secretary).

REPERTOIRE BOOKS
There is a considerable amount of saxophone music in print. Much of it is listed in the following reference books:

Woodwind Solo and Study Material	Voxman, H. and Merriman, L. The Instrumentalist Co., Illinois. 1975.
Woodwind Ensemble Music Guide	Voxman, H. and Merriman, L. The Instrumentalist Co. Illinois. 1973.
125 Years of Music for the Saxophone	Londeix, J. Leduc and Co. Paris.
Jazz Reference and Research Materials	Meadow, E. S. General Publishing Inc. New York. 1981.

REFERENCES
1. Horwood, W. W., *Adolph Sax 1814-1894. His Life and Legacy,* Bramley Books, Hampshire, England. 1980.
2. Kennedy, M. *Elgar Orchestral Music,* BBC London 1970. (Quote as from P.12 in 1975 reprint).
3. Londeix, J. M., *125 Ans de Musique pour Saxophone,* Leduc and Co., Paris, 1971.
4. Horwood, W. W., Op. cit.
5. Weisberg, A., *The Art of Wind Playing,* Schirmer, New York, 1975.
6. Brown, J. R., and Charleson, B., *Front Line Sax Solos* Chappell Music Ltd., London, 1979.